The Hopi Way

An Odyssey

THE HOPI WAY

AN ODYSSEY

BY

ROBERT BOISSIERE

Sunstone Press
Santa Fe, New Mexico

FIRST EDITION

Printed in the United States of America

Library of Congress Cataloging in Publication Data

Boissiere, Robert, 1914 –
    The Hopi way.

    1. Hopi Indians—Fiction. I. Title.
PS3552.0'556H6   1985   813'.54   84-16256
ISBN: 0-86534-055-2

Published in 1985 by SUNSTONE PRESS Post Office Box 2321 / Santa Fe, New Mexico 87504-2321 / USA

This book is dedicated to the memory of

LESLIE KOYAWENA, long time friend and Hopi brother,
and PAUL COZE, without whom I would have never known
the joys, the promises and the values of
THE HOPI WAY.

Author's Note

Throughout this book, the name CATCINA, also spelled KAT-CHINA, will come often. A Catcina is the representation of the spirit entity of a person, an object or an animal. It is personified and impersonated by a male member of the Catcina clan or Catcinup.

It is said by the Hopis that long, long ago, the spirits themselves came to the villages, but today the people have lost the ability to see them, so they are impersonated by members of each village.

Catcinas are said to have their spiritual home in the mountains above Flagstaff (Arizona) called the San Francisco peaks. It is from there that every year they come to visit the people at the Hopi villages from November to July, performing Catcina ceremonies to answer their prayers for joy, health, happiness and good crops.

Catcina dolls are carvings of the beings given to the little girls at the villages during a Catcina ceremony.

R.B.
April 1984

The author at the Hopi village of Shipaulovi, Arizona.

Foreword

I dedicate this book to the Hopi family who long ago accepted me as their brother. In more than thirty years this relationship never faltered.

Although all the names are fictitious, the Hopi locations in this book are real, and the family life of Sarah and Stewart and their children is based on fact. I have attempted to depict, as accurately as possible, the struggle for survival the Hopi people demonstrate while maintaining their true identity after four hundred years of subjection to *savage intrusion;* first the Spanish and, later, the incredible pressures of the white industrial world.

Nevertheless, in a most miraculous way, four hundred years since the first Spaniard appeared on the horizon, the Hopis not only have a culture of their own, but surprisingly are the keepers of a way of life that large nations could learn from if they were to last as long as the Hopis have.

THE HOPI WAY

An Odyssey

The bright orange half globe of the rising sun was just appearing on the thin line of the horizon when Sarah Pamosi opened her eyes from a long restless night on the couch. Long accustomed to rising as the Sun Father was sending warm rays toward his children, Sarah awakened the moment the first sunbeam hit the wall beside her.

Stewart, her husband of twenty years, had come home late Saturday night, which was the night before, ever since he had found work at the Winslow depot. Drunk again, he came in loud and stumbling. He and his white friends always celebrated the end of the work week in town, drinking. Sarah worried when he came home like that; she thought about how he might have fallen asleep at the wheel.

It had not always been this way. But it had been worse since sending the children to school. The extra expense was too heavy for the family; Stewart needed the job in town. Farming his ancestral fields would not provide the cash to clothe and feed the children, get a truck instead of the old wagon or burro, simply stay alive in a more complicated world.

She slept poorly on the couch, without her husband beside her. But the pervasive smell of liquor on his breath was worse — she could not stand it!

As Sarah drew her dress over her slip, she looked through the window. The sun, projecting its oblique light on the intensity of the Hopi desert, was sending good thoughts into her heart. Since she was a little girl, this sight, every morning, filled her with joy.

Hopi houses, hers in particular, stand at the edge of a precipitous rocky ledge on which the village is built. Crowning the vertical wall of perhaps a thousand feet, the view through the window of desert expanse is unbelievable for anyone not raised on an eagle's nest — for this is what Hopi villages really are — perched on top of high rocky mesas over the desert floor of northern Arizona.

Dressing herself, looking through the window, Sarah's mind was far, far away...what changes there were in her life. So hard to raise a family, so many fancy goods needed at the store down below. Stewart brought his check to her almost intact. There was, of course, the expense of all that liquor...

She remembered as a little girl, her mother sending her to the only store, the Shipaulovi Trading Post, a very tiny little store built on the Mishongnovi ledge by the only road connecting the village to the outside world.

It was seldom that she was sent for coffee, flour or sugar, but she loved running down the rocky trail by the kivas. The store goods were fascinating; candies wrapped in colored papers, cookies in cellophane wrappings. Her mother always gave her just the amount necessary for a purchase so she had to content herself in only looking. Every once in a while the storekeeper, old man Secakuku, would give her a candy that she would consume on the way up so her brothers would not take it away from her.

In those days little girls wore black mantas (homespun pueblo dresses) almost exclusively, one for everyday use, and one for the feast days. With bare feet and her waist tightened in the green, red and black ceremonial sash of her people, Sarah knew happy times where wants were limited to what the fathers and grandfathers brought home from the fields. The store was another world.

For treats they had sweet melons her father grew in his fields several miles away from the mesa. There he walked, or perched on top of his faithful donkey, rode every day to attend his crops. Sweet corn, especially the early ones, satisfied her sweet tooth. Baked in a big hole in the ground by the field, husks on, and dried later at the village in the sun, the sweet corn indeed lived up to its name.

There were less worries then — or so it seemed. No one went to town very often; there were no roads to speak of, just sand trails. Now the blacktop road to Winslow was an hour's trip. Back then it took a whole day.

All of this was going round and round in her head as she finished dressing; her eyes moved dreamily along the distant rises of the Hopi buttes far away, at the very edge of the desert.

The boys were sleeping on the roof these last days of July. Too stuffy in the house they said. Besides, up there, next to the eagle, they felt free, just as if they were eagles themselves, ready to take off a thousand feet above the pink, yellow and blue desert below.

Pauline and Alice were awakening. Sarah could hear their voices from the little storeroom behind the blanket serving as a door to their makeshift bedroom.

It was Sunday and perhaps the *Catcinas* would dance again in Mishongnovi, as they often did when they felt the people wanted them to, even after they had danced all of Saturday. There was good reason, it being the last dance of the year. *Niman* is the *Catcinas'* annual goodbye after which they go back to the San Francisco peaks, their ancestral home, until next year.

"Come on, girls, time to get up. I need help preparing breakfast."

Silence answered their mother's call to duty but a few minutes later, from under the old blanket, the puffy faces of two girls made their appearance.

"What do you want us to do, Mom?"

"Bring some dry sweet corn from the back room. I'd like to steam it for breakfast; we have some stew left from yesterday."

Soon the coffee pot spread its aroma through the house, giving everyone the zest to start the new day. Outside the back door, in the little courtyard, Tsokavo and Suma folded the mattresses they had used that night on the roof.

"Suma, do not forget to feed our brother eagle, Kwahu. He should be fed first so he can bring us a good life," Sarah reminded them.

While the noises of breakfast went on, Stewart was deep asleep, quite undisturbed by anything.

"Isn't Daddy going to eat with us?" Alice asked.

Sarah did not answer as it would not have been proper to say something nasty in front of the children.

Everyone sat silent at the table (as was custom), faces close to the bowl in front of them, each child absorbed in thought. The first meal of the day was a silent meditation, a prayer, a greeting to the new day but also to the memory of the departed ones who have become "cloud people."

Imperceptibly (only eyes accustomed to Hopi ways could have noticed) Sarah Pamosi, mother of the family and, under matriarchal law by which Hopi social life is ruled, master of the house, gathered a few pieces of food in her hand and swiftly threw them under the table. This sacramental gesture, as old as the Hopis themselves, signified the living family feeding the departed one, the ancestors to whom the living feel deeply united.

"Mama?"

"Yes, Kotsamana."

"Mausi and I are going to watch the dance at Mishongnovi after breakfast."

"Be sure that your bed is made. And pass the broom here, we might have visitors later. It is Sunday, you know."

The girls obediently ran to their room. What their mother told them was law.

Doing the dishes again, Sarah's mind went far away, lost itself in the immensity of the desert. In better times, Nonantiwa — her husband's Hopi name which she liked better than the Anglo Stewart — would have been at the table with them instead of sleeping off the morning in a heavy stupor. She missed him, she missed what he had been, what she had fallen in love with; his strength, his ability to grow beautiful corn, delicious melons.

Now, he would spend half the day sleeping, and tomorrow before sunrise he would go to work again. In the meantime, they might exchange not a single word.

She could not help it, she knew she was blaming *Pahana* life (white people's culture) for the damage done to their ancestral way of life. They were so much happier before.

"Okay, Mom, we are ready to go now."

Pauline and Alice were dressed neatly and very attractively in their colorful cotton print dresses, beautifully washed and pressed. Pauline had her long jet hair caught in a single fat braid on the side, her bangs almost to her eyes. She looked both pretty and mysterious. Alice kept her hair loose, neatly trimmed; although only fourteen, she looked as big as her sister.

"I know you are going to see Makto," Sarah said to her eldest daughter. "And I know you are promised to each other, but remember that you have to keep his respect. Talk to him only when people are around, do not look in each other's eyes — it is too soon."

"Oh Mom... things are different now. It is not anymore like when you and Daddy got engaged. You know, it's like they do on TV."

"Yes," Sarah said bitterly, "just like they do on TV."

The two girls went away laughing, their moccasined feet ready to run down the trail by the kivas, the short cut to Mishongnovi.

In the distance, the muffled beat of the drum the rhythmic tonality of the *Catcinas'* rattles, kept the beat of the *Catcina* song. It could be heard in both Shipaulovi and Mishongnovi. Even if they had not been at the dance, they were held in unison with the messengers of the gods. By the sound of the song alone, as it echoed from boulder to boulder across the abyss which divided the two villages, they were united and at peace.

Grunting noises, like a bear coming out of his den, signified to Sarah that her husband was coming to life. In another moment he was on his way to the coffee pot.

"I am getting ready to see the *Catcinas*," Sarah said to him. No answer.

After a couple of cups of coffee, Stewart said to her, "I am going to check my fields see if my corn is all right."

My poor husband, Sarah thought, he is bewitched by liquor and he can't help it... only in his fields does he become himself again.

It was so different twenty years ago. He was courting me then and I had to invent all kinds of excuses for not spending the whole evening at home, doing my chores or making baskets. I was living with Grandma and she was trying to train me to become a good Hopi wife. My thoughts were seldom on my work. All I thought about was getting out of the house to see Stewart under the cover of that old lover's accomplice, night, just as my daughters do today when they sneak off.

My heart was beating hard under the black manta and the shawl I casually put on my shoulders. I didn't want Grandma to think I was anxious.

— I am going to visit with Aunt Martha in Mishongnovi, I would tell her.

Grandma knew her sister had gone to bed hours ago but would say nothing, perhaps because she, too, remembered the excuses she gave to her mother.

Stewart waited patiently by the Peach House, one of many small stone houses used for storing fruit in summer, which was at the edge of the mesa overlooking the desert. He was looking out over the edge at the sparkling lights of the trading posts down below when I came up to him. Safe and secure, at last. How deeply in love I was, how much in harmony we were with each other.

I remember later, after we were happily married, Stewart's mother took ill, very ill. It was the illness the white doctors at the agency hospital call cancer. She got so weak the Keams Canyon Hospital transferred her to Gallup General Hosptial for treatment.

Stewart was very close to his mother. She had raised him by herself after his father had been killed when a horse kicked him in the head.

In those days, the trip to Gallup was a big distance. Hopi and Navajo roads were few and far between, and Gallup was a hundred miles away. We had no truck then, just a horse and light wagon, so we walked from our mesa top down to the main road where the Secakuku store is now.

A Navajo family visiting relatives in Tuba City was returning home to Window Rock. They stopped their truck and gave us a ride. We felt good. We would get to Gallup in one tenth the time it took us in our wagon. We had dried peaches and dried meat for Grandma. We did not know she would not be able to do more than look at them.

The Navajos let us out at Window Rock, twenty-five miles from Gallup. We were hungry and we made camp there for the night. We built a fire and laid our blankets out under the stars. The big window in the middle of the cliff above us sparkled with stars — all of them farther away than on our own mesa top. But the cool desert air after the hot day brought us close together under the blankets.

I could tell how badly hurt Stewart was over his mother's illness. The last of his family leaving him. I wanted to love him, seeing how hurt his eyes were, how slowly he moved and spoke. In those days, before the children, he was my gentle giant, and the sweet smell of his body and the dry sage under the moon, made us forget our troubles.

— "Stay close to me, Sarah, I am scared," this Stewart said to me the next morning when we faced the hopsital we had heard so many bad things about. The elders in the kiva warned us not to go near it.

Stewart said to me: "I have not always been good to my mother. As a young man I took her for granted. I missed my father. Sometimes I drank Pahana liquor and made trouble for her. Maybe it is my fault that she is in this Pahana hospital."

"No," I said, "she is here. That is all. It is your duty, now, to be a son to her as long as she lives. You can do no more. Thinking about it is bad."

After a while we went inside. Stewart held on to my arm and stayed very close to me. He seemed to have lost his voice.

The sun was high when Sarah put the key in its usual place so anyone from the family could come in if need be. "The *Catcinas* will be coming back from their lunch pretty soon," she thought.

"Sarah! Are you going to Mishongnovi?" One of her neighbors called.

"Yes, Lucie. Let's go."

Throwing colorful shawls on their shoulders, the two Hopi ladies headed for the trail that climbs down toward Mishongnovi. The desire to run down those big steps cut from rocky ledge was too strong to resist, and they skip-hopped like a couple of children.

Then up the steep incline leading to the other village plaza, where the long line of *Catcinas* was starting to pour into the village courtyard from the other end. With her Hopi sixth sense, Sarah had timed herself perfectly. After the noon recess, the tall masked beings were preparing for the first afternoon ceremony, arms filled to capacity with food the ladies of the village brought them. In a long, ceremonial line, the ladies had stood and made their offerings while the *Catcinas* rested in the sacred cave under the village, taking each parcel as it came.

This immense collection of breads, fruits, melons, cookies, pies of all shapes and colors made a huge pile next to the main village shrine. A roar of approbation came from the whole village whose assembled members now greeted the *Catcinas* heartily.

Several rows of benches and portable chairs were placed by the members of the houses facing the long rectangular center. Guests from some of the other eleven Hopi villages, family members, white friends, Navajos and also members of some Rio Grande pueblos, in all, a thousand or more people, stood or sat entranced in the four entrances of the village center. Four or five rows of spectators standing on the roofs of the houses made an incredible array of shawls, red bandanas, blankets and cowboy hats.

On the roof tops, the first row sat on the fire walls letting their feet dangle over their friends underneath. There was an incredible feeling of expectation and excitement in the air, and then, all of a sudden, there came the murmur of waves upon a shore, and the rattle of the leading *Catcina* signalled the line of thirty-six messengers of the spirit world to move.

All noises coming from the crowd stopped at once. The attention of everyone, as if suspended in midair, made for a mystic moment of silence. Time and space vanished as the sacred creation began.

Exploding into great waves of sound, the long semi-circular line of *Niman Catcinas* began to sway and move like a feathered serpent; forward and backward, downward and upward in the intricacies of Hopi song created expressly for each ceremony never to be repeated again.

The moccasined feet struck the earth all at once, causing the turtle shells, attached to the right leg of the *Catcinas* just under the knee, to sound like the rasping of the sacred snake.

Two Hopi priests, bare chested with heavy turquoise necklaces clinging from their necks, shouted sacramental phrases, urging the *Catcinas* to sing and dance. From a small leather pouch, the priests poured cornmeal upon the *Catcinas'* left shoulders, blessing them in the name of the village that hosted them.

The figures of these two old men with their flowing shoulder length white hair, and wearing only *Pitchcunas* — white handwoven kilts of native cotton with red, green and black Hopi ceremonial designs on the right sides — were most impressive.

Each *Catcina* wore the same identical kilt: a long decorated sash hanging on the right side, a wolf or coyote pelt hanging from his back, fresh branches of green spruce stuck underneath the sash to signify the *Catcina*'s everlasting spirit.

The upper parts of their bodies were painted black with two white spirals, and they wore turquoise necklaces with turquoise bow guards on the left wrists. Their masks — nearly three feet tall — rested on thick collars of spruce. At the top of these masks, the white and black tail feathers of an eagle gleamed in the sun.

The sight of the dancers impersonating the divine messengers was incredible. The superhuman appearance of the figures called *Hemis Catcinas*, performing the *Niman* ceremony that day, made Sarah's total being vibrate with pride. Forgetting now her sad thoughts about Stewart, she transcended all, finding her place in a glistening and sacred world brought forth by the Spirit Messengers, the dancers flashing before her.

For a time, along with the hundreds surrounding her, she traveled to a different plane. The dimensions created by the sacred beings is more of heaven than of earth.

After the ceremonial dance was performed four times, in each of the four sacred directions, the *Niman Catcinas* threw gifts at the crowd. Truly, an extension of heavenly bestowal, the *Catcinas* would return again for dances lasting a whole day, sunup to sundown. And they would have armfuls of *Catcina* dolls for the little girls of the village, and beautifully decorated bows and arrows and rattles for the little boys.

Sarah prepared to leave the crowded courtyard just before the throngs dissolved and the people regained the privacy of their homes. Turning, she saw Kotsamana and Pauline who had cornered Makto, her boyfriend.

Makto, at eighteen, was a strong well-built Hopi youth whose black hair fell to his shoulders. He had an aura of well-being, calm serenity, unusual qualities for one so young.

Sarah could tell that Pauline was asking him to accompany her somewhere because his eyes were either drawn to the ground in front of him or staring at the sky in the respectful way he had been taught to conduct himself.

"What did Makto say to you?" Sarah asked her daughter back at the house.

"Oh, nothing, Mom. I'll see him tonight."

Young Hopis who are in love are strictly controlled during the day but at night they are free to be together in the intimacy of long hours spent on boulders and terraces below each of the villages.

Often the girls are with child by the time a formal Hopi wedding is performed. But by practicing marriage beforehand, sometimes even within the framework of family living, the girl sizes up the qualities of her future husband as a provider, father and companion.

Often the girl changes her mind when she discovers the boy does not have enough of what it takes to be the head of a family. Then she and her family will raise the child, now a full member of her family, until she finds a proper companion.

Was I careful enough to follow the teachings of the Old Ones? Was I watching Stewart to see if he would make a good husband? Was I only having a good time? Stewart was a good lover, always seeing that I had pleasure before himself. But — if I had paid more attention to what was happening, I would have seen his weakness. He is still a good provider, but he would be far better off without his drinking habit, without his constant — what was it? The death of his mother in that hospital was part of it. He blamed himself, he would always blame himself.

So the elders were right. They were always right: to feel the prongs of desire and the pleasure that goes with it does not promise a good husband. It takes a good farmer, a good worker, a man without fear to do that. I was lucky. If Stewart had been worse I would have had to come back home and raise my children with the help of my parents. Stewart was good enough, that is good enough for me.

The Hopi method of betrothal is as ancient as the Hopi themselves.

"It is going to be time to send some *piki* to Makto's family," Sarah said to her daughter. *Piki,* a wafer bread made of blue corn gruel, is batter-baked on a hot stone. Used as a gift on ceremonial occasions, in this case, *piki* would tell Makto's family that Pauline's parents had accepted her husband.

"Oh Mom! Not yet, it is too early."

"Too early! Do you think I am blind. I can see you are with child."

"So what, I am just not ready yet."

"Kotsamana, a Hopi wedding takes a long time, we should start early." A Hopi wedding, in fact, takes years; its intricate giving and paying back ceremonies urged Sarah to hasten the matter.

"Besides," Pauline retorted, "who told you I wanted a Hopi wedding?"

"Kotsamana!" Sarah answered with some anger showing in her voice. "I had a Hopi wedding, your grandmother had a Hopi wedding. You cannot be married like a *Pahana,* by a priest or a judge. The old ones among the cloud people would be angered; it would mean bad luck for your marriage."

Pauline threw herself on the couch in front of the overworked and ultimately ignored TV set. Disturbed by her mother's words, she crossed her arms over her chest in defiance. Then, lacking self-confidence and fearful of confronting Sarah, she dropped this pose and took up nail-biting instead.

A Hopi wedding, a Hopi wedding. It will last for years — so much money, so much trouble. All the giving and receiving ceremonies, the paying back forever. I'll be making plaques and baking piki until I am a very old woman. My girl friends in Phoenix went to a judge, and it was done: onetwothree! None of this Hopi intricacy. But maybe that isn't right either. Who remembers a onetwothree ceremony? Maybe, I could do it both ways...

"Mom, why do I have to get married the Hopi way?"

"A Hopi wedding," her mother answered calmly, "develops as the husband and wife grow into it. Like life itself, it is long and sometimes tiring. It is also complicated, but then life is too. The Mud Fight, the *plaques*, the *piki* — all of it makes for the good life, the right way. That is the Hopi Way. I learned this from my aunts and grandmother: life can be very dangerous. In our practices, doing everything exactly as it was always done, there is discipline. In discipline there is faith. In faith there is no danger. That is the way it is."

"But Mom, it takes forever," Pauline drew out the last word to emphasize her impatience.

Her mother ignored the remark and went on with her talk.

"Just as our people plant corn and grow corn, we plant and watch a family grow. Our ceremonies guarantee the father and mother of the Catcinas will watch over us, give us their support and protection. There is no hurrying the Hopi Way; *Pahanas* rush through everything. They have not finished one thing before they jump to another. In the correct ceremony of family life, you will get to know your husband properly. You will know your responsibilities. You will become guardians and teachers of your own little ones. If you are careful you will not make foolish mistakes. That is the Hopi Way."

As her mother finished speaking, Pauline felt ashamed of herself. She looked down at the floor. In her own sudden impatience, she had questioned something that was beyond question. She knew now that the teaching of her elders awaited her, and that she must be ready for it. Her girlfriends in Phoenix could never cast away doubt in the way she could. Gone, like a pail of water off the cliff beyond her door.

But would it come back with the wind — would the *Pahana* wind blow it back in her face?

Although Pauline knew that the sure way Hopis plant and grow corn, they also plant and grow a family — in the traditional way — she did not feel the necessity to abide by it herself. Still, she did not want to anger or upset her mother, and she knew that to go against her will, and that of the Hopi way, could be harmful.

"I have to start preparing supper," Sarah said. "Your dad is going to return from his fields. I see the sun is starting its trip for the other side of the earth.

"Kotsamana, please set the bowls, forks and coffee cups for supper. Your father will be hungry and will want to go to bed early. You know he must leave in the middle of the night to be at the yard in Winslow by five a.m."

Without saying a word, Tsokavo, Pauline's brother, and Suma, his younger brother, came in through the back door, tired from a full day of *Niman Catcinas*, heading straight for the television set.

Leaning on the table, Stewart willed his sleeping, dazed brain back to life. He sipped his coffee slowly. His mind, as it awakened, seemed to go off away from this world, this place, this time. He felt it whirling away from him like Kwahu, free of the rooftop at last. He was back in time, back in his cornfields.

How beautiful the squashes, the melons. How perfect. There is no television set in the cornfield. Father Sun shines down upon the green leaves and gives his blessing. At night when Father Sun has gone to the other side of the sky, the kerosene lamps flicker in all the houses. Light enough, light enough to talk by. Then to sleep. Now, in these bad times, nobody sleeps anymore. Now, the TV set tells me when to go to work and when to come home. The TV set takes electricity we don't need and we don't want and makes us go to work to pay for it. And now, the TV set and the voices piping in it, tells us to send our children away to school. For a hundred years this TV set waited to do this. For a thousand years we had no TV set, no city schools to send our children to, no bills to pay for things we never wanted to buy. But then there were Pahana troops who took our great good parents into camps far away and kept them there to teach us how to behave so that we would forget the Hopi Way and prepare our minds for the coming of the TV set. But the damage is done and it is too late. the TV set has won. At sixteen my son Tsokavo should be in the kiva learning how the Hopi Way is done; instead he has to be in Phoenix learning how the Pahanas came out of their dark ages to rule the world. And with the help of the Hopi Council, the Indian Bureau in Washington brings water to our village and builds frame houses on the desert floor — electricity, running water, telephones — where will it stop? So what if it is easier on the Old Ones to live down in these tract homes? How do we pay for it with money we do not have? Easier, easier, easier, this is how the Pahanas triumphed over their dark ages, the easiest way is the best way, not the Hopi Way which has always been hard, harder, hardest . . .

Pushing himself away from the table, Stewart got up, opened the back door which led to a little courtyard at the edge of the cliff. A low wall was all that kept his children from falling off the abyss. Yet, they did not fall. A fantasia of desert shape and color awaited Stewart's eye. He rested his hands on the wall; once it was the Hopi protective wall against enemy raids, wave after wave of outsiders, discoverers who wanted in. Now the wall provided no more protection. Things came in that walls couldn't keep out. And where would it stop?

The television was a strange newcomer to most of the Hopi homes. It came when electric power came as a complimentary gift from the white culture. However, since the programs were for white viewers and the themes estranged from Indian beliefs, the television sets in most of the mud and stone houses played to no one except the grey-blue shadows dancing on five hundred year old walls.

The boys watched in disbelief at the glamorous expression of Hollywood's golden years. The smooth sound of a Glenn Miller tune filled the old dwelling.

Sarah sniffed the air and knew her eldest boy Tsokavo had been drinking, probably with some of the others off away from the dance. It was happening more and more, a habit they picked up in school, in Phoenix.

Ancestrally, at sixteen, Tsokavo would have been extremely active in his *Catcina* training, since his initiation into the cult took place when he was twelve. But being in high school in Phoenix most of the year interfered with his Hopi teaching. His ways were as confused as Glenn Miller's music on the mesa top, where, hours earlier, the beat of a drum had commanded everyone's attention.

KIPOK CATCINA
War Catcina Leader

S tars studded the Arizona sky this late July.
Pauline, when darkness came, skipped away from the house, her slender body wrapped in a warm shawl to shield her from the wind.

Makto and Pauline had several favorite spots for their noctural encounters, but she had suggested meeting tonight at the sacred spring which suggested to Makto that it was going to be a very special night.

There were several sacred springs near the villages, each one serving a function in relation to ceremonies; this one served primarily the rituals conducive to family stability, health, fertility.

A good mile or mile and a half from the village, the sacred spring was hidden among monumental boulders which, at night, took on all sorts of incredible shapes: monsters, giants, lofty peaks, some friendly, some unfriendly.

Pauline walked briskly among these fantasies of the night, anxious to meet Makto, imagining his stance among the rocks above the spring as he stood tall against the night sky.

It took her twenty to twenty-five minutes to reach the place, and she felt herself running down slopes and up others with the same light step her mother used in going to the dances.

Makto's slender body imprinted itself like a decal against the moonlit sky. Pauline shivered slightly at the sight of him; the expectation of meeting her lover in circumstances older than either she or her family, as old, perhaps, as the rock she walked upon.

Above the spring a little rocky trail made steps to the boulders above. Pauline climbed on light as a feather.

Slowly, in feline gestures, the two lovers met and began to blend into the hunchback shadows of the spring. As their bodies pressed together, Makto and Kotsamana entered the age old ritual of re-energizing the earth, and for a moment in eternity, a second of time, the two Hopi lovers gave sense to man's presence on this planet. An intense current went through them and into the earth on which they were standing. Then Makto and Pauline sat respectfully on the rocky monolith, feet motionless in space, the sacred spring shining below them. They saw the moon and the stars ride upon the still waters. They saw their reflection, ghostly, watery, unalive but still living.

"Makto," Pauline said at last, "the time has come for us to seal our love forever. For us to live together as man and wife. This is the way I feel. Do you feel the same way?"

For a while Makto was silent, weighing the answer that was either to join or undo what they had been doing for months.

"This is why you wanted us to meet at the sacred spring tonight?" Makto asked.

"Yes."

"My answer is yes. We will join permanently, and give protection to our children."

"So you know?"

"I have known for some time that our first child is to come."

Falling into each other's arms, Makto and Kotsamana now sealed the promise carried by their feelings over the long months. The greatest ceremony of all had been performed in a matter of seconds.

"Let us get married right away," Pauline said.

"How can we do that? Hopi weddings take a long time."

"We go to Winslow tomorrow and get married at the Justice of the Peace. That's the way we can do it."

Makto looked at Pauline in shock, but he remained silent, disbelieving her words.

"You mean to have the white man look into our affairs?"

"We can have our Hopi wedding later," Pauline said placatingly, "but this way we can live together and our baby will have a home."

"We can have that the Hopi way. We can live in your house until I build you one. The way our forefathers have done it we should do it, too."

Pauline could not refute Makto's thought which was also her mother's. However, the two years spent in the white high school in Phoenix had taught her other ways than those of her people. Makto had never been off the reservation. Her mind was now in two worlds and she felt the very ground beneath her reverberate with her own indecision.

She started crying silently, the confused hurt rising from deep within her.

"Kotsamana, don't cry!" Makto had never seen Pauline cry before; now the feeling of pain was his also.

"All right," he said soothingly, "don't cry anymore. We'll go to the white man's town, but under one condition. Promise me we will be married the Hopi way."

Pauline nodded twice, her eyes beautiful with the shine of her tears.

NATA-ASKA
The Black Ogre

Summer and warm weather went by so fast that school time was again facing the Hopi family. Sarah was unprepared to face the necessities that went with it.

Pauline and Makto had moved in, and the prospect of a new baby was a blessing for everyone but the autumn school needs made Sarah worry for there was so little money to go around.

One Sunday afternoon Stewart returned from the fields with the two boys. They brought melons and late blue corn, a pickup full.

"That is everything," Stewart told his wife. "Nothing like when I could spend all my time in my fields, but it is something."

"Thank you, Stewart. I know you are doing your best. Perhaps it is not like in the old days when we were young and first married but I have enough blue corn I think to make the *piki* and *pikami* to pay back Makto's folks for their gifts. What I am worried about is sending Tsokavo, Mausi and Suma to school."

"I thought you made a basket for that!"

"I did. It was an order for those white folks in Wisconsin. They wrote a month ago saying they could not pay for it before next January. They said I should sell it to someone else. I have not been able to. You know it is a big basket."

"How much were they going to pay for it?"

"Two thousand, but I am going to try to sell it for twelve hundred dollars now. We need shoes, dresses, shirts and pants for all three children."

Stewart sat down near the TV which flickered in the dark. He seemed crushed by the effort of a day in the fields joined with the prospect of their financial needs.

"I'll see in Winslow," he said, "if I can borrow from the finance company; I pay already for the truck and the ice box out of each pay check. Still they might do it."

"Try, Stewart, try. For the children."

"I wish that white schooling would not cost so much. In the old days Hopis taught everything their children needed to know at home or in the fields. Everybody was happy and it cost no more than passing on the secrets of life. We were our own guardians then."

"Times have changed."

"The sun goes by in the sky the same, the moon watches us sleep, the stars tell us to go to the kiva, all the same."

They looked at each other with great apprehension and sadness in their eyes as if something they could not quite comprehend was over them, pushing their spirits lower and lower until there was no way to stand straight and tall.

Borrowing more money got Stewart thinking of Ralph and his family, how he had come to him when he left for the Grand Canyon the morning of the Snake Dance three years ago. "I am leaving for the land of our ancestors," he had said. What had he meant by that? For a long time Stewart thought Ralph was talking about the Sipapu, or Place of Emergence of all Hopis, for the Grand Canyon was that place. But as time went on, Stewart realized Ralph was saying something else to him.

I remember the day Ralph got the new GMC pickup truck: hard, dark metal shining in the sun. So they would have no more traveling or hauling difficulties. But then Ralph explained how he bought it — through the same finance company that held me in its claws. That was okay, Ralph said. He could live with it. What he could not live with, later, was the day his son, Frank, drove the pickup home from Winslow, got drunk with some other boys from the village, drove off the top of a dry wash. The new chrome and metal machine carried all those boys to their deaths thirty feet below.

Ralph changed after that. He drank, he said, in honor of the death of his son. Hopis do not talk like that; Ralph was telling a fib. It was telling the Pahana lie better than the Pahana could tell. And now the finance company demanded its money for the wrecked pickup. This was something any Indian, anywhere, could not accept. Ralph felt he had already paid the devil's price. But in the white world, business does not accept or excuse emotional suffering, bad luck, disability. The price is always the price. Ralph did not understand how the Pahana world had already made itself at home in Hopi land; indispensable the Pahana way was now, confusing wants with needs, complicating tribal life; with each move in, it owned a little more of the Hopi soul. So when Ralph said he was going to the Grand Canyon, I was glad for him.

A week later his body was at the bottom of a canyon, in the murky waters of the Colorado. Through the mighty corridor of the canyon he, at last, found peace.

But there was no peace any more for Hopi. Stewart was resigned to it.

So as the page of the month of September was turned on the calendar above the TV set, Tsokavo left for the Phoenix Indian High School with the other boys and girls of the village.

Sarah saw them go with sadness in her heart. What they were learning in the government schools did not help to be Hopis. It was just the opposite; full of confusing thoughts, they were trapped in the old and the new and the just begun, and they did not know how to be with any of it. They watched it go by, and their lives were poorer for watching and not living. Like the phantoms in the television set, the children threw ghostly shadows on the walls.

Sarah knew some of the money she gave her son would be spent on liquor or buying "weed" which made them forgetful and sleepy, and turned them away from the ceremonies.

Mausi and Suma were still at the elementary school below the village and were home every day. But plans for a Hopi high school on the reservation were only talk and so the school in Phoenix took the older ones and kept them, and there was nothing to be done about it.

Fortunately Suma was going to be "initiated" in the spring. Becoming a *Catcina* would keep him away from the temptations of the modern world. By then, perhaps a high school would be built at New Oraibi...

SIO SALAKO
Hopi Zuni Shalako

SIKYAHOTE
The Yellow A'Hote

The first pangs of the early frosts reached the Hopi mesas in mid-November. The first *Catcinas* made their appearance on the mesas bringing the good news in the villages that a new ceremonial year was about to begin with *Soyal* and "new fire ceremonies."

One Friday evening Stewart came home from work early.

"My husband, you are home one day ahead of time," Sarah said. "What is the matter?"

"A meeting of the Hopi Council tomorrow," Stewart replied.

"Oh, I see...you mean the alcoholic meeting."

"No, not that. We have to vote on the Hopi Cultural Center which is to be built near Shungopovi."

For months Stewart had attended the tribal alcoholic recovery program at Sarah's insistence. Some happiness had come to the family on the heels of it.

"Do you remember Mr. Bryson from the Bureau of Indian Affairs?" Stewart asked his wife.

Sarah nodded yes.

"He will stop here tomorrow to pick me up for the Council meeting."

"I bet he wants you to vote for the project."

"My feelings are mixed about it. In a way I could see how it could help the *Pahanas* who are always wanting to visit us in one place. They call it a Cultural Center, this place which will have a restaurant, motel, and shops to buy things."

Sarah exclaimed. "But it will be in the midst of our villages, right on top of Second Mesa!"

"Worse," Stewart added bitterly, "this center will sit on Uncle Leslie's bean field.

"I have heard the other men talking. The Kikmongwi of our village will advise us to say either yes or no."

"He is only the ancestral village authority. Others will have their say, you can be sure of it."

At noon the next day Philip Bryson knocked on Stewart and Sarah's door.

Stewart immediately invited him to sit down and eat something with them, for this was custom, a traditional greeting.

"I came early," the BIA official stated, "I thought we might talk here better than in a moving car."

Philip Bryson spoke with the ease of one who hands out orders and sees them swiftly carried away by a busy and obeisant staff. Utterly unaware of the effect of his words, in English, to a Hopi audience, he spoke to them as he would to anyone in his large and efficient office. The fact that the Hopi tongue is a richer and more imagistic language than English had never occurred to Bryson whose brisk dealings with the Indians were formal and without any particular feeling on his part. But then none of his dictates imparted feelings, unless he found certain quality remarks to be useful to his purpose as an administrator.

"I want to tell you," Philip Bryson mused off the cuff, "that I am quite proud of my record with the Hopis..."

Sarah prepared the table in silence, letting the man's odd use of personal pronouns sink in. *He* was proud — was it for him to say, or even think such a thought?

He went on: "...I helped bring electricity, running water, toilets, central heating to you people..." Bryson allowed a small silence to pass between this thought and the one coming: "Such things," he add-

ed philosophically, "must truly enhance your lives." Another respectful pause, more for his own benefit than his listeners'.

Sarah and Stewart said nothing.

"A Hopi Cultural Center, as proposed by my department to the
Hopi Council will make a big difference to the economy of the tribe."
Bryson went on, "The restaurant will employ Hopi people, and the
museum complex will make tourists better acquainted with Hopi
customs and history."

"May I ask," Stewart said in a soft voice, "what your department
is. I am not familiar with the BIA."

"Your question is perfectly legitimate," Bryson answered smartly.
"I am exclusive director of building projects and architectural designs
for the area controlled by the Phoenix office. The Hopi Reservation is
under our control. The Hopi Council — being the federal government
-recognized-and-supported governing body of the Hopi tribe —
naturally is my first promotional target. I would like it very much if
you would back me on this."

Sarah placed a big bowl of mutton stew on the table where they
conversed. Next to it she placed a steaming pot of coffee and a basket
of Hopi bread. "Please eat," she said, and took her own place at the
table.

For a while they ate in silence, as was custom, Sarah and Stewart
delicately dipping fingers into the stew and eating, Mr. Bryson using
his spoon. He was uncomfortable with the silence and attentiveness to
eating. He was used to a constant stream of conversation while he ate;
this unnatural way of using fingers in stew and not saying anything
unnerved him. "Tell me," he asked, no longer able to keep quiet, "I
wonder, Sarah, if you would permit me the privilege of knowing your
opinion in this matter Stewart and I have been talking about."

The right of head of the household allowed a Hopi woman the
complete and dominant role in the household and other personal mat-
ters; meetings, however, were men's work. It was highly unusual,
especially at table, for a Hopi woman to voice such views as applied to

Council or other governing affairs. But the right to speak out, in this context, since she was asked by an outsider, was hers and she quickly seized it.

"Your work for us has been commended by yourself already," she said, smiling sadly, "but I commend you for it also. Mr. Bryson, I don't think you understand the difference between us Hopis and the people in your world. We are a small desert people. You are rather large, and not of the desert."

Philip Bryson showed color in his face for the first time in many years. For a moment he wanted to dip his fingers in the stew. His eyes very briefly surveyed the portly heave of his belly, and he wondered if her comment had anything to do with his being overweight.

Sarah continued: "The Hopi people have a long acquaintance with the desert and its ways. When it is harsh, we know how to deal with it on its own terms. But what we can't seem to do, any of us, is agree on how to deal with your terms."

Philip Bryson colored again. "You don't seem to understand," he coughed nervously, "I merely represent our government, just as Stewart here may represent his, or yours. You see, the Hopi Council only implements our policies when it feels it can agree with them."

"That is our problem, Mr. Bryson," Sarah said. "We don't agree among ourselves. The Hopi Council is evenly divided as to the legitimacy of the Council itself. Many Hopis claim they have not been consulted on it. Our traditional form of government is through village chiefs who discuss the needs of the people with the people. This has been going on for a very long time. So, to change this traditional form of government to a new form handled by a tribal governing body that represents the whole tribe is convenient only for your friends in Washington. For us, it is harsher than the desert is for you."

Philip Bryson stopped blushing. Now he knew just what he was dealing with — a very worthy and articulate opponent to his aims.

"In what way," he asked in a mock humble tone which only he knew he was using, "do you think we might better our position?"

Sarah answered with implacable feminine logic: "By using the chiefs and the clans to make our decisions, with us and for us. Our fathers far back in time gave us sacred land. The borders are the Grand Canyon, the San Francisco Peaks, the Kaibab Mountains, and far down to the ruins of pueblos in Mexico. These are all ours, and we must take care of them in the Hopi Way."

Stewart had been politely listening the whole time his wife spoke. There was little or nothing for him to add. She had spoken wisely. His only regret was that she would not be allowed to make such talk in Washington where it would truly do the most good. This man, Bryson, was only a small feather in a big ceremonial bonnet.

"Well, then, I thank you both for the pleasure of this delicious lunch," Philip Bryson said unctuously. His plate, which Sarah and Stewart both avoided looking at, was hardly touched. He had, she thought, eaten only words for lunch.

"Before I leave, Stewart, there is something you might explain to me. In all my time dealing with you people, I have never quite understood the difference, politically speaking, between Old Oraibi and New Oraibi."

"New Oraibi," Stewart explained, "is a rather recent village while Old Oraibi claims to be the oldest of all the villages. The split was caused by modern-thinking members and traditional ones, just as there are today. This happened in the twenties over such things as electricity, running water, toilets and central heating.

Their violent beliefs were finally settled in a very ancient way: one faction trying to push the other over a line drawn on the ground. Those who wanted to stick to the old ways lost and had to leave the village the same day with whatever they could take with them. So they traveled west and founded the village of Hotevilla, then Bakavi and New Oraibi below the Mesa."

KOYEMSI
Mudhead Catcina

Pauline helped her mother all the time now. She was getting bigger as the weeks went by. Makto, busy with *Catcina* "doings" (as the Hopis themselves call it) was, nevertheless, quarrying stones from the mesa rock bed to build a house for his bride and his coming family. This he did in his spare time.

Sarah mentioned to Pauline: "You have to help me sort blue corn so I can make *piki*. The time has come to pay Makto's family back. But first I must finish your wedding plaque to put the *piki* in."

Plaques are basketry made by Hopi women in the shape of a large plate, ceremonially woven and decorated with grass and yucca strips for the purpose of offering gifts.

"Oh, Mom, there is no hurry."

"What do you mean, no hurry? The gifts we received have to be answered. You still seem in no hurry to get married, how come?"

Pauline was visibly embarrassed by her mother's question.

"Mother, I can't hide it any longer from you. I have to tell you the truth, no matter how difficult it is for me."

Shocked by her daughter's answer, Sarah stiffened and formally beckoned Pauline to sit down next to her.

"You see, Mom...Makto and I...are already married."

"I don't understand."

"I just couldn't wait for a Hopi wedding ceremony. It takes so long, so...Makto and I went to the JP in Winslow."

Sarah took in every bit of this new affront to her senses.

"How could you do a thing like that? Did Makto agree?"

"Only to please me, Mom. Please don't get angry at me, at least I didn't go to see a priest! But I thought it was best for the baby, that's what I learned in school"

"Well, it's done," Sarah said, letting it go quickly, "But you must also have a Hopi wedding."

"I promised that to Makto."

"I can see now why you were not in a great hurry. It's all right, Kotsamana, I understand. I am your mother."

The complete truth established between them, the two women looked at each other and smiled.

(Making PIKI, the ancestral ceremonial bread of the Hopis, is an intricate and very involved operation. The PIKI house is a room usually located in the very back of the family adobe, very small most of the time, one of the original rooms of the village built perhaps centuries ago. It is a very magical place, feminine domain, the rafters and the whole ceiling, in fact, darkened by smoke to a crisp.

In a corner is the PIKI stove, a piece of flat basalt perhaps one and a half feet wide by two feet long and two to three inches thick. It stands on two flat erected stones, providing a space underneath for the fire. The whole place gives the feeling of the magical and comforting cave so often imagined in everyone's psyche as the place of beginnings.

When the stone is hot, a light batter of blue cornmeal and ashes mixed with water is spread by the one making the PIKI (in this case, the mother of the bride, after dipping her bare hands in the batter.

The light film of blue corn meal mixture cooks instantly and is rolled before it dries. It looks like a paper or papyrus roll. Sometimes color is added to the batter, creating incredible combinations of yellow, red and blue PIKI assortments.

Usually several ladies come to keep company with the PIKI maker, telling stories that men are not supposed to hear...it would make them blush! PIKI rolls can be piled up several feet high and kept in cardboard boxes until enough of them are made to pay back for the gifts received by the bride's family.)

"Your uncle is coming tonight to pick up the white cotton for your bridal ceremonial robe. He will start it right away. He told me he just finished making his loom today."

(Uncles are generally chosen to weave the Hopi bridal ceremonial robes. To that effect, they build the primitive looms out of small logs, usually in their secret little room in which men do their ceremonial work such as making CATCINA masks or weaving which is a man's prerogative.)

It will be months before Kotsamana will appear garbed in the white nuptial robe, white tall boots of doeskin and black manta of the Hopis. Her face will be painted white, and in her arms she will hold another robe identical to the one she will be wearing. This second robe will be in a container made of willow twigs tightened together, and she will eventually be wrapped in it when her life ends. She will be buried in it for her trip to the cloud country, where cloud people live.

It was toward the end of that month that Kotsmana had her baby. A beautiful little boy that her matriarchal aunt named Little Bear during the name giving ceremony in which the newborn is presented to the rising sun for the first time.

SOWI-ING CATCINA
Deer Catcina

It was a sunny, Saturday morning in early March when the village woke to the eventful mood that precedes a special event.

Sarah, Pauline and two of Sarah's sisters had baked part of the night: cookies, breads, cakes, pies, the whole gamut of culinary skills of Hopi ladies.

A very special ceremony was on its way, one that would bring the village into a tight family, shutting out the rest of the world. Isolated, proud, self-sufficient, the Hopis liked this time when all ties with the outside, all problems of survival in the complicated world of the whites, suddenly disappeared.

Hopi reverted to Hopi for itself. *Soyoko* was about to make her appearance going from house to house, pressing everyone hard, admonishing children and parents alike to be good or to pay the price. This was the reason for the baking, the excitement, the feverish preparations.

Everyone was tense, nervous and apprehensive. *Soyoko* is a powerful *Catcina*. Some might say the dark side of the Great Mother. *Soyoko* is feared and respected because she teaches the Hopi way.

The morning passed with baked delights going from house to house. Their makers, who had worked all during the night, ensured every house would be well provided for. It was necessary to give *Soyoko* more than she would ask. Otherwise she would take children with her long white hook, roast them and eat them!

It was around noon when the first rumor of *Soyoko* reached Sarah's house. Most of the village children, followed by a few adults, spied some fifteen *Catcinas* lined up in front of a house below the mesa next to the old store It was Lucie's house the *Catcinas* were besieging. They would be up at Shipaulovi in half an hour or so.

The atmosphere of the village was tense, and mounting. Children were running after each other, knowing that in a few moments, they would have to be inside the houses well away from *Soyoko's* reach!

Using the steep grade of the short cut to climb to the village, stopping in its kivas to deposit the mountains of goodies collected at each house as a token of good behavior, the long file of the *Catcinas* moved gracefully in their extravagant garb.

Soyoko, the old ogre lady with black mask, black manta and white boots, had a sack on her back and a long white hook in her right hand with which she would catch the children, if she were not provided with all she asked for.

Next to her, all in white, were two representations of *Massau,* gods of the earth, followed by a fantastic array of mixed *Catcinas:* ogres with long snouts carrying long knives, swords, saws and making awful noises, frightening the villagers into a state of caution and respect; whipping out with lassos at those who would dare to come too close to this awesome group of representatives of the spirit world.

"What is it you want?"

Sarah opened the door, hearing the knock of the *Catcinas;* they struck the wood with the hook designed to catch little children.

Suddenly she was face to face with the hideous black face of the *Soyoko,* red tongue hanging from a mouth ringed with painted teeth.

"I came to punish children who have been bad during the year," *Soyoko* said.

"We don't have any such children in this house," replied Sarah.

"I know better," the persistent *Catcina* continued, and she made an attempt to get in.

"Wait, wait a minute," implored Sarah. "All night we baked for you, cookies, pies, bread."

As Sarah spoke in the ritual way formulated for centuries upon centuries, Pauline and Alice passed her the pies and cookies.

"Meat. We want meat," yelled all the *Catcinas* in unison.

"We need meat," emphasized *Soyoko*, "otherwise we take the children, roast them and eat them, because of their bad deeds during the year."

At that instant, Pauline brought Sarah a huge dish of mutton stew that she gave to *Soyoko's* helpers.

"That's better," she said.

Their arms loaded with food, the fearsome group of *Catcinas* started toward the kiva where other piles of food were accumulated.

"Kua Kuai, Kua Kuai," exclaimed the *Catcinas* who expressed their thanks in all sorts of comical ways.

Furtively, Sarah closed the door to everyone's relief.

"Ah. It's over," Pauline sighed, throwing herself on the couch.

From behind the couch two of Sarah's *Pahana* lady friends (who had witnessed the whole ordeal) slowly arose. Terrified by the appearance of the fearsome group of *Catcinas,* these women had been chased throughout the village while the *Catcinas* tried to lasso them. Finally, they took refuge in Sarah's house, slipping through the back door.

"Sarah, how can you stand for all this," they said, still pale from their experience. Sarah, Pauline and Alice burst into laughter.

"We are used to it." she explained, "We have gone through all that since we were kids."

"But, what's the purpose of all that scare?"

"It is the Hopi way of atoning for mistakes accumulated through the year; it gives us a chance to pay, as Christians put it. I think you call it confession and communion. You make offerings to God and his helpers, the same as we do. Later today, we will all share the food after it has been blessed by its passage throughout the kivas. It's the same as yours, only we are doing it the Hopi way."

By two in the afternoon, it was again safe to come out of the house without risking *Soyoko's* wrath; those children, who were so unfortunate to be taken to the kiva until ransom could be paid, were awaiting their release.

"Let's go to Hotevilla," Tsokavo suggested, staring blankly at the TV.

"What is going on?" Sarah asked.

"The *Catcinas* are going to have a big parade. The second 'bean dance' they are having this year."

"All right," Sarah conceded, "Let's all go!"

"Not me," said Stewart, his usual coldness putting a damper on everyone's enthusiasm. "I have to help in the kiva."

It was not very long, however, before Sarah's family had piled into the family pickup (Stewart's pickup, as Hopi custom has it) and were headed to Hotevilla, the main village of the third Hopi mesa. In the 1920s, following a long and intense political fight which divided the people of Old Oraibi, the village had split, and the losers relocated to Hotevilla.

Tsokavo had to park the truck almost at the entrance of the village, near the main road. Hundreds of cars and vehicles of all sorts blocked their path.

"Look at that!" Sarah exclaimed, "*Pahanas* everywhere. Let's hurry so we can find a place to stay. Auntie Emma has her house right on the plaza, we might make it to her place."

In the distance the sound of drums and loud shouting of *Mudheads* did not drown out the ritual chanting of the *Catcinas*. Again, the spectacle revealed row upon row of colorfully attired Hopis and their visitors from the ground floor of the village courtyard to the top of the roofs that bordered it.

Perhaps two thousand people were there, forming a huge amphitheatre. Right at the center of it, a chorus of at least forty mudhead *Koyemsis* (the Hopi word for clowns) were involved in ritual singing. Next to them, single file, two *Kwahu Catcinas* and two Butterfly

Maidens stood motionless. In contrast to the mudheads' boisterous behavior, the magnificent tall *Catcinas* seemed like gods fallen from the sky.

Kwahu is the Eagle *Catcina:* huge wings of eagle feathers, tall blue and black mask topped by the orange tail feather of a tropical macaw. The *Polikmanas* (Butterfly Maidens) displaying a white face mask with triangular hachured areas and red spots on their cheeks, their chins painted with lines radiating from the mouth and each triangle painted with a different color; on each of their heads was a tableta one third their size elaborately painted with Hopi sacred colors, covered with beautiful eagle-breast feathers. They were wearing ceremonial embroidered robes and Hopi kilts worn like a blouse, and red, black and white maiden shawls. Their feet were bare, painted yellow.

The courtyard of Hopis and visitors showed their respect with reverent meditative silence. In the distance, other groups of mixed *Catcinas* projected their fantastic garb against the sky, as they went from kiva to kiva. Another world; another life; Hopi at its best.

Kua-Kuais and *Asqualis* (Hopi male and female thank yous) filled the square.

The dances, alternating all afternoon, were only a prelude to what would happen all night in the village kivas, what is commonly called the "night *Catcina* dances," part of the *Powamu* cycle or ritual.

"Come in and eat!" Auntie Emma called to her relatives, piled up in rows in front of her house. In they came to share the huge bowls of mutton stew. The meat was cooked with bean sprouts which were grown in the kivas and distributed by the *Catcinas* only in the morning. The sprouts were part of a communion ritual reverently observed by the entire village during its second "bean ceremonial."

Sarah and her brood waited quietly inside to partake of the ceremonial meal that binds families from one Hopi village to another (there are twelve in all).

All of a sudden, without warning, the *Koyemsis* stopped singing and, in a split second, they were bombarding the entire crowd with apples, oranges, candies, popcorn balls, etc. All kinds of projectiles were finding their marks. All hands were ready to receive them, creating a furor of noise.

Sarah and her family were back at home by six-thirty that evening, in time to get ready to go to the Mishongnovi Kiva Night Dances where many of their relatives would participate. The Shipaulovi Night Dances would not happen for another two weeks.

"Mama, I want to stay home tonight."

"Alice, you have to come with me to the *Pumpkin* kiva; it is our duty. It is your father's kiva, you know."

"I know, but I am tired."

Her two brothers could not contain their sarcastic laughs.

"Alice, you are too young to go at night and meet the boys below the mesa!" Alice could not fool her mother because Sarah remembered when she was the same age; the thrill of personal freedom calling more strongly than a communal dance event.

It was not until eleven p.m., after having spent almost an hour piled up against the *Pumpkin* kiva side door in the cold February night, that Sarah, Pauline and Alice finally found a seat and waited for the first group of *Catcinas* to come in.

In the dim light of the kiva, Sarah could see that the large underground dwelling of prayer and worship was crowded with Hopi women and children.

The tall, heavy ladder which went to the opening of the roof of the kiva separated them from the area where the *Catcinas* would be dancing, there were stone benches and a wooden floor used as a resounding board like a drum.

At the front of the ladder, the kiva priest and his helper smoked a sacred pipe, and waited to bless the first group of *Catcinas* to enter the kiva.

The acrid smell of sacred tobacco, the dim light of the kerosene lamp, the intense heat and smell of the potbelly coal stove, gave a feeling of being in the belly of the earth. Soon the *Catcinas* prancing on the kiva roof would call down the gaping kiva hole to ask if they might bless the people by their presence.

Feelings were reminiscent of Christmas Eve, weddings or high mass. The reverence, the spiritual participation and understanding were total from both adults and children.

As teams of *Catcinas* succeeded each other through the night, Sarah heard her *Pahana* lady friends among the crowd of Hopi women, exchange impressions in low, measured voices so as not to be heard.

"Isn't it strange to watch the relationship between these figures of the heavenly messengers and the people?" one said to the other.

"Yes," she said in a muffled voice, "to me they look like ancient gods descended from an Olympian domain. I find it highly mystical — this mixture of intense religious fervor and rhythmic fascination in the sacred songs, the intricacy of the footwork, the magic of the out-of-this-world costumes. It projects mind and soul toward the Creator as I never experienced before."

Sarah listened to this objective account of her religion with amusement. They mean well, she thought, and what they do not understand, they do not mock.

What Sarah knew above all was that words were boxes that trapped thoughts. These *Pahanas* were trapped in the little boxes of their thoughts. To see and to hear was enough.

Zuni *Catcinas*, Navajo *Catcinas*, long-haired *Catcinas*, Supai *Catcinas*, Comanche *Catcinas*, velvet-shirted *Catcinas*, succeeded each other, moving down the ladder, one after the other. The dance continued into the wee hours of the morning, when, finally, after the dances had been done, the families found their way along the rugged paths of the mesas below the crowded sky, which guided them home.

Hopi days are very long days, but Hopi nights can be very short. Sarah hid herself under the covers, close to the warm body of her husband, hoping to catch enough strength for the coming day.

"Did you see Tsokavo after the dance this afternoon?" Sarah asked.

"I haven't"

"He has worried me lately," Sarah said. "Have you noticed the change in his manner since he has been going back to the school in Phoenix?"

Stewart answered with a sigh, "Boys go through all kinds of changes when they grow up."

"I know about them. I don't mean normal changes, Stewart. We must not forget what happened when he was ten."

"I remember that fall very well. He was climbing the cliffs with his friends. What has that to do with it?"

"Everything. The *Pahana* doctor who examined him said that our Tsokavo had experienced a concussion that would cause him trouble later when he was older."

"You never told me this. Did the doctor tell you what kind of trouble would visit Tsokavo?"

Sarah tightened her lips, as if to hold back the awful truth of the thing. She did not want to burden Stewart with more than he could handle. The boy was very special to him, and she could not afford to have Stewart worrying all the time and wondering if his son was going to be all right.

"We don't have to talk about it now," Sarah pleaded.

"I want to know," Stewart said crossly, "what is this thing you have been keeping to yourself?"

"It would happen any time. Under stress, the doctor said, that would be the time when it might be worse. Blackouts, he called them. Times when Tsokavo would not see anything. Oh, Stewart it's too awful to think about: our boy, blind."

"So that was the deep dark secret. The *Pahana* doctor doesn't know everything. He knows only what he knows, and I think that is very little. Tsokavo has never had one single blackout. Not one, in all these years! What does he know, this doctor who doesn't even know our son."

"I was afraid you would be angry. You would not let it go."

"There," Stewart said impatiently, "I have let it go," and he raised his hand above his head and pretended to release a bit of fluff with his fingers.

Sarah sat up in bed, her face drawn and pale in the half light. "Stewart, there is more. He drinks and he smokes with his friends."

"Other boys his age pressure him into it. All of them experiment with things. And soon tire of them, too."

"But Stewart, our Tsokavo is different, that is what I have been telling you. He is different because of that old injury. The other boys can go get drunk, but when our boy does it, he has those blackouts the doctor told me about."

"What makes you so sure?"

"He told me. Stewart, Tsokavo told me he had them."

SNAKE DANCER
(Not a Catcina)

May brought warmer and sunnier days to Hopi. The nights were warmer, and in the fields, everywhere, the gentle green sprouts of the early corn, squashes and beans told the people that Mother Earth was responding to the prayers all winter in the kivas.

From the top of the mesas, where the villages sleepily observed the greater life which surrounded them, patches of green appeared every day. Fruit trees, mainly the old Hopi peaches and apricots, once brought to the people by the "padres" following the heels of the conquistadores, were in bloom, adding their sweet fragrance to the gentle awakening of the season.

Sarah, Pauline and all their relatives had been dancing on the mesa tops in preparation for a great event. Great Uncle Mark had nearly finished the weaving of the wedding robes. Gifts, offerings and presents had all been answered, for now the time had come for the most distinctive parts of the marriage ceremony.

Feverishly, in Makto's mother's house (still, in a way, his own, until he finished building his bride another one) for weeks now, pickup after pickup brought sack after sack of flour, sugar, coffee, corn and rice. Today three more "pickups-full were waiting so that relatives from both sides gathered to unload them.

The main room of the house was stacked to the ceiling. A human chain of twelve relatives took the sacks of flour, sugar, beans, breads, cakes and pies and completely filled the whole of the large room that was Makto's family house.

A lot of it would be used for the wedding feast, at which, not only Shipaulovi people would come, but families from other villages too, hundreds in all; but these goods were also intended for the bride to start her new family life — perhaps the remnant of an old custom where among Indian tribes the groom had to "purchase" his bride.

PALHIK MANA
Butterfly Maiden

Pauline, it's time to get up."

Still very early, the sun not yet up over the village of sleepy people who, for weeks, had worked way into the night in preparation for this wedding.

"Remember, Pauline, today you have to go to Makto's house to grind corn."

"Yes, Mom, I know," Pauline answered, yawning.

It was the promise of a beautiful day for Pauline, a hard day too, for she would be spending it mostly on her knees, grinding sacred corn in her future mother-in-law's *Piki* house; a day spent in prayer as she would bend over the grinding stones reflecting on her coming change of life, her coming child, and the coming-together of Makto and herself.

Sarah stepped outside, and in the still dim light of the bright new day, the San Francisco peaks shone in the first rays of the rising sun far on the edge of the desert. She went up a few steps of the ladder going to the roof.

"Suma," she called gently to her younger son, "please get up; I need your help."

"Yes, Mother. I am coming."

Like all the boys his age, Suma was spending his nights on the rooftop close to the stars, thinking about his own initiation this spring.

"My dear son," Sarah told Suma as soon as he entered the house, "take some of these buckets and make mud for me. Your aunts are going to be here pretty soon for the mud fight."

It was perhaps ten-thirty or so when several of Pauline's aunts came to pick Sarah up. The sun was already warm, the May sunlight glaring.

"Let's go," said the eldest of the Hopi ladies.

They were wearing the oldest clothes they could find. However, they were still clean and freshly ironed.

Spirits were high among all the ladies as they started toward the house of the groom's mother, each one carrying two buckets of freshly made mud.

They barely had arrived when the eldest of the bride's aunts started slinging mud at the house doors and windows, signaling the start of a Hopi wedding: the mud fight.

As if waiting for the given signal, all aunts from the groom's side came out of the house — as if the tiny little house had suddenly exploded — and in an instant ten or more ladies were throwing mud at each other in dead earnest. Soon, none of them was recognizable, each covered with mud from head to toe.

Some of Pauline's aunts had entered the house during the melee, throwing mud all over the main room's walls, windows and floor. Of course, the room had been emptied previously in order to let the ceremonial mud fight take its course, as each side seemingly emptied its frustrations and built-up anger. This was a good way to clear tensions that had grown during the protracted weeks of preparation for the marriage ceremony.

"Let's clean up the mess," one of the aunts said laughingly to the others. Jokes and fake insults had flown back and forth for more than half an hour, and now, precisely as it all started, the clean-up began on the inside of the house. The outside would have to wait for later because Sarah and several relatives were already bringing in food for the feast.

"Help me spread the tablecloth," Sarah said.

She had thought of everything, and in what seemed only an in-tant, the hard-packed mud floor was freshly cleaned, covered with a huge sheet, loaded with dishes full of hominy, stew, bread, chili, and all sorts of breads and sweets.

The hungry mud-fighting ladies greeted it all with obvious signs of joy and satisfaction as they sat upon the floor, as if nothing had ever happened.

"Let's eat," said the eldest of the matriarchal corps of elders of both families.

"Let's eat," everyone repeated in unison.

HÓLOLO
(no English translation)

Unlike all other ceremonies that punctuate mesa life, the ceremony of marriage brings with it a magic that is unique among all peoples of the earth. Hopi is no exception, although the unusual length of the whole ordeal, that can sometimes last five years or more, in ceremony after ceremony, makes it special among all other tribal events in the human family.

The presentation of the bride, the first time she wears her wedding robes in public, is the culmination of the ritual, which, in itself, lasts several days.

Tension had been building for weeks in Sarah's house, and it was definitely showing on everyone, especially Pauline. Being the center of attention for such a long time was a strain on her, particularly because the Hopi way contrasted dramatically with life at the Indian School in Phoenix.

For months now she had been called by her Indian name, Kotsamana, and it seemed to her that she was living with a new self, one she did not know much about. The traditional ways of the Hopis contrasted so much from the casual ways of the *Pahana*, which some part of her had found to be agreeable.

She realized more and more now, that she was becoming a wife and a mother, that the mystery and mastery of womanhood would link her life to a greater and more mystical union with an outer and inner world she had previously known nothing about. At times, it was more than she could grasp.

In its proverbial wisdom, the Hopi way and its long succession of ceremonials and rituals had been both a comfort and a guidance, a help she discovered as she went along, the depth of it centering her personality not upon herself, as it had been, but upon the totality of her people. Especially valuable was the knowledge of other women who had gone through it before her, giving her a deeper sense of the lives of others. The personal, therefore, was binding her to the impersonal. It was a holiness she felt, like having been chosen to host the very current of life itself, using her body to perpetuate the subsistence of humanity as a whole.

Slowly and majestically, the Sun Father was rising at the limits of the Hopi horizon far away to the east on this glorious day that found Sarah's household busy preparing all the garments and the sacred effects the bride was going to use during the day.

Indeed, it was a very special day as it coincided with a great ritualistic event for the whole village as the Hopi *Shalako*, one of the most sacred *Catcinas*, mother of all, was to make her appearance that day in Shipaulovi.

The bride would be presented alongside her to the entire population of the expanded village, enlarged ten times by visitors coming from all the other villages; this was the Hopi way.

"Mausi! Suma! Please help put cups, spoons and bowls on the table so we can have a quick breakfast. We have so much to do." Gently but firmly Sarah urged everyone to share the necessary preparations.

Both Stewart and Tsokavo had arrived late during the night from Phoenix and Winslow to be part of the great event.

On the big bed on the back room where Pauline and Makto had lived for months, the white robes, tall white deerskin boots and all the accoutrements the bride would wear during the day were displayed ceremoniously. Everyone approached them with reverence because these would make her holy during the ceremony.

The feast to follow the bride's presentation to the *Shalako* would be held at the in-laws' so none of that had to be faced by Sarah whose responsibility lay solely with the bride.

Sarah's mother and several aunts came early, partaking of coffee, bread and cookies.

The grandmother, eldest of the household for the extent of the day, and much loved by everyone, would assume a prominent role in the succession of events beginning with the dressing of the bride and the fixing of her hair.

In the matriarchal society of the Hopis, such a day revolved around the home and the respect of the female. The male role was very much in the background; they tried to help where they could in ordeals quite different from those to which they were accustomed.

Now that breakfast was out of the way, all the women and children assembled in Pauline's room, forming a half-circle around Pauline who was seated in a chair.

Sarah's mother, Martha, gave instructions to everyone in the form of a long litany resembling a prayer or poem.

Some were to fix the bride's hair, for the first time, in two *changos* of the married woman status — no longer would she wear it in the butterfly style of the Hopi maidens. Someone else was to fix Alice's hair and Sarah's hair, all three to be dressed in Hopi ceremonial attire.

Then each one would be helped into her ceremonial black 'manta" and sash with white, black and red hand-woven shawl, unique to the Hopi.

"What time do you think it is?" Sarah asked her husband who was respectfully watching the ceremony at a distance with his two sons.

"It is going to be eleven pretty soon."

"It is going to be time to go to Makto's house soon," Sarah said with a tinge of anguish in her voice.

One of Pauline's aunts had already painted the bride's pretty face with the white chalk found in the secret place for that purpose, and now, dressed in her Hopi clothes, the time had come to put the large hand-woven white robe on her shoulders, the big white tassels on each side slightly touching the ground.

"Is everyone ready?" the eldest of the aunts asked authoritatively.

Now, slowly, in a procession-like manner, the bride walked through the village on her way to her in-laws.

Pauline was indeed a majestic figure, holding her sacred bundle in her extended arms, as she walked with measured steps through the village. Her mother at her right, her sister at her left, three figures of ancient Hopi design doing what had been done before any of them were born.

Behind them the rest of the party followed, Stewart and his sons carrying gifts of food for Pauline's in-laws.

As the bride entered Makto's mother's house, his relatives blessed her with prayers, sprinkling her with cornmeal; then they sat her in the main room among themselves believing that her holy presence would bring ultimate happiness to their home.

"Suma, go and watch when the *Shalako* is to arrive in the village and come back to let us know," Sarah said to her younger boy.

Waiting for the great *Catcina* to come, the large bridal party now made up of the two sides of the family, meditated in silence on the spiritual event which was taking place.

Even the children were silent, all their attention concentrated on the white figure of the bride, immobile, eyes fixed on the ground before her.

It was not too long before singing could be heard.

Entering without noise, Suma shyly stated, "They are here."

The bride was led out, followed by her lady elders, and the men surrounding Makto who was dressed in his most festive clothes.

Slowly, in a most humble way, Kotsamana followed the intricate pattern of the small streets leading to the village central square, everybody trailing her.

All of a sudden, as she turned into the small alley opening onto the huge space in which all the major village gatherings took place, she faced the multitude of villagers several rows thick around the plaza and rooftops.

The great moment in which the bride finally shows herself to the entire village had arrived. Here she claimed her bridal status for everyone to see.

At the moment she took her place in the front row of the spectators, alone, protected solely by the intimacy and power of the white bridal shawl which covered her from head to toe, two ten-foot tall sacred Hopi *Shalakos* (*Salako Taka* and *Salako Mana*), male and female, appeared on the opposite side of the rectangular courtyard.

The moment was awesome. This moment, in time, a mere spark in the eternal succession of sparks, suspended itself and filled the consciousness of every living being.

Surrounded by perhaps twenty-five of the mystical Hopi *Koyemsis* (mudhead clowns), the two *Catcinas* made their way to the center of the plaza preceded by two *Catcinas* that always accompanied them, protectors who never stopped dancing.

The gigantic size of the *Shalakos* — the costumes, made of black and white eagle tail-feathers, a gorgeous display in itself, turquoise and silver necklaces on top of one another, a light pink mask decorated with stripes of all different colors, the whole monumental figure covered by an elaborate *tableta* ringed with the fluffy breast feathers of the eagle.

Surrounding the drummer pounding on an oversize drum, more than fifty *Koyemsis* surrounded the two tall *Shalakos*, as if trying to protect them from possible damages resulting from their encounter in this physical world of humans. The rhythm of the mudheads' high pitched song and the fast steps peculiar to their society made the air ring, vibrating with wholeness.

At the extreme opposite end of the village central square, the silent solitary figure of the Hopi bride stood motionless.

After the gigantic figures, clad in their golden eagle feathers, returned to their Olympian home of the San Francisco mountains, the bridal feast began, as both Sarah's and Makto's sides of the families fed anyone and everyone who felt like honoring the bride by their presence. Hundreds of people pressed upon her. However, her cerremonial duties finished, Pauline relaxed by helping to feed the guests while she responded to the greetings of the multitudes who attended the bridal feast that lasted all day long.

SALAKO MANA
Hopi Female Shalako

Two o'clock in the morning the smooth surface of the paved road from Winslow to Hopi was a long black ribbon in the full moon. The night of his sister's wedding, Tsokavo and his friends chose this surface for a game as dangerous as Russian roulette.

Slipping away from the feast in the late afternoon in Stewart's truck, Tsokavo took the flight of his dreams all those long evenings while away at school: a joy ride. In Winslow they tanked up on gas and booze, knowing full well that back at Hopi such an endeavor would cost them dearly. But here in Winslow no one would know.

Three of them sat in the front seat on the way home, sipping tokay. Tsokavo drove with a feeling of exhilarant speed, and the more he drank, the more he believed this was the ride of his life. He felt like a warrior of old, riding his war horse to death. He felt the power of the machine merge triumphantly with the fire of the sweet liquor in his blood, and he pressed the accelerator ever downward amid peals of laughter from his friends.

Then suddenly there was silence in his ears, a roaring silence like that of a waterfall he once heard, deafening. Then the black ribbon of highway began to darken and fill in the edges of his vision and the roar of water in his ears grew louder. Willy, sitting next to him, shouted for Tsokavo to get on the right side of the road, but he could not hear him. Willy grabbed the wheel and jerked it back, the truck veered, lurched toward the shoulder, spilling tokay all over the three boys.

But Tsokavo was not there any more. As the truck plowed out of control, driving off the road and deep into the stillness of moonlit desert, Tsokavo saw nothing and, like the parable, heard nothing, said nothing. Neither of the other boys saw the small smile creep over his lips. It was a Hopi smile, conceived in Hopi thought when death is near — when death is not to be sought or bought or fled from, only to be greeted with open eyes, eyes that do not see a black road or white sand, milky in the moon.

The impact was instantaneous; the truck sang like a bullet into the rocky wall of the dry wash, made vertical by countless flashfloods that raced between its banks. The shock catapulted Willy and Kern into the ceiling of the cab, breaking their necks simultaneously. Tsokavo, however, felt himself lifted off his seat gently, as if in a deep and wonderful slow moving dream.

In a fraction of time, so fast it cannot be recorded, I see myself as a child, then at the day of my initiation when my ceremonial father tells me to follow the middle road, the way of moderation and balance, the Hopi way. I know that, now, it is impossible to maintain the wishes of my ceremonial father — too late.

Tsokavo's head passed through the windshield of the truck, the balance broken, the middle way destroyed.

The last thing I see is my father holding his hand out to lead me into the softly cushioned land of the cloud people. I want to go.

It was somewhere between one and two in the morning of the next day when Sarah heard a truck stop in front of the house, a most unusual occurrence. A gentle knock on the door got her up in no time. She opened the door and glanced at the small rocky terrace lit by the bright moonlight. Then she saw the truck and she knew... The horrible truth hit her right in the chest, her heart felt like it had stopped. Walking toward the flat bed of the truck, she saw him — Tsokavo lying there, cold and frozen, dead.

She broke into a terrible spasm, tears choking her. The two men who had brought her son's broken body helped her get back in the house. Emotionally, it was as if a tornado had hit the house.

Stewart, who had not yet gone back to work after the wedding, was in total shock and despair. He helped the two men bring his son's disfigured and limp body into the house and laid him on the bare floor of the main room.

Almost without consulting each other, everyone knew immediately what to do. The men moved all the furniture into the other room, leaving the room in which Tsokavo's body was lying completely bare.

The women, who now numbered eight or ten with family and neighbors awakened by the tragic circumstances helping, washed and dressed the body, all in almost complete silence. In less than an hour, Tsokavo lay there covered with ceremonial blankets, ready to be blessed in the Hopi way.

It was later that night as Stewart and the other men finally grabbed some coffee and bread that they finally learned the terrible truth.

"We were coming back from Winslow," the two men began, "when we saw this truck wavering on the road coming toward us. It almost hit us. We stopped and looked back and that's when it happened. The truck missed the small bridge and fell head on in the wash twenty feet below..."

The men's recollection of the accident fell in the heavy silence of the broken hearts. It was easy to tell what was in everyone's mind. A beautiful young life had been snuffed out in an instant. The old white man's firewater had done it once more, throwing an entire family into despair.

In a deep grave voice, Stewart started to talk in Hopi. "Our beloved son has rejoined our ancestors in the land of the cloud people. We know that from there he will join them in sending good moisture for our fields and happiness for the people. He will watch over us like the eagle that leaves after the *Niman* ceremony in July. We were not given the opportunity to prepare him to take our gifts to the Great Spirit along with him, but we know that before life was taken out of his body, he must have thought about it.

"We send our blessings and our prayers so his spirit will some day come back as the *Catcina* that he never was down here because of the government decisions to send our children away from our own ancestral teachings, to learn their way although we know that the Hopi way of learning is best for us."

His eyes misted with tears, the father blessed his son's body with the sacred cornmeal that accompanies Hopis in whatever they do and wherever they go.

The death of Tsokavo had brought despair, confusion and doubts on the very sunset of Pauline's wedding. More than ever, Sarah, Stewart and their chldren felt the need to shelter themselves within the womb of their Hopi beliefs, of ancestral customs and teachings that had been especially designed through the centuries for people who had settled in the midst of desert conditions, unique at least in North America. They were a desert people, nourished by a desert land and led by the Great Spirit represented by *Masau*.

Long ago the Hopi prophecies foretold the painful circumstances of their present day life and the influence on them by a strange people they didn't know then. They knew now but more than ever, it was essential for all of them to withdraw within the nurturing beneficial effects of their own culture in order to survive through the cataclysmic events predicted by their ancient teachings.

Perhaps without realizing it, Sarah and Stewart were looking at their younger son Suma whose initiation into the *Catcina* clan was near, the event that might trigger this complete return to the Hopi way that above all would be able to heal so many years of hardship and erring in a style of life that was not in their best interests.

Pauline was now married to Makto, well-trained in his ancestral Hopi way of life and as a farmer; the land would sustain them. Tsokavo had gone to the cloud people and they would live their lives now.

Suma would be initiated in the *Catcina* society, giving everyone the opportunity to find strength from the deep and nourishing pit of ancestral Hopi ways.

PANG CATCINA
Mountain Sheep Catcina

He stood in the doorway framed by sunlight, holding a small porkpie hat. With the sun behind his rather massive head, Philip Bryson looked monolithic, a statue of white mortality. Nothing would affect the pleasant man who dispatched unpleasant orders; he was for all time, like the televisions he sanctioned, like the running water, the shopping carts gleaming in the sun down below the mesa.

"I have come on behalf of my department to express our condolences on the death of your son."

"He was buried yesterday," Stewart said without emphasis.

"I want you to know how sorry I am, personally, for what happened. Yet, I feel obliged to add that this again illustrates that driving and drinking do not mix!"

"Federal law does not forbid it — only Hopi law," Sarah said. "They do not drink here, on this mesa, because they are not allowed. In town, anything goes. You know that yourself."

Stewart added, speaking from experience: "They go to town because someone is willing to make a couple of bucks off some dumb Indian."

"I think," Bryson said judiciously, "that alcohol education, if you want to call it that, ought to be initiated in the home. Then the boys would know what they are up against."

He cast a wary eye in the direction of Stewart to see if this remark had any effect. But as far as he could tell it didn't. Stewart returned his gaze with a level stare that said nothing.

"The damage of alcohol..." Bryson began, but Sarah cut him off.

"I think," she said, "enough has been said about the dangers of drinking."

"I'm sorry if I..." and she cut him off again.

"As far as our son is concerned: it happened, it is done, finished. He is in the next world already. One day he will come back like our ancestors did. Then he might find a new earth, one that is governed by moderation, and not pickup trucks or tokay wine. Where the cloud people lie, there are no pay toilets, Mr. Bryson. No Hopi councils either. All is as it should be."

Then she paused, aware of the spell her words had cast over the two men who were amazed by the precision of her voice and thought.

The sun coming in through the half open door sent an even blade of gold light into the dark shadowy room. In the sun shaft, dust motes dances. Sarah, standing half in and half out of his blinding sunbeam, said matter-of-factly: "A time will come when harmony will follow the present state of confusion; then life on earth will align itself with the other side where the cloud people have their home and where my son is now."

NAVAN CATCINA
Velvet Shirt Catcina

The *Catcinas* went back to the San Francisco peaks at the end of July. Autumn had come and gone as the days shortened, and the daily trip of the sun in the darkness of the night on the other side of the earth became longer and longer.

It was now *Powamu* again, and the *Catcinas* had reappeared on the mesas, bringing their yearly message of hope for good sustaining crops and a good year for the Hopis.

One step at a time, Suma had followed for a couple of years, all the different steps that a Hopi boy has to take in order to prepare himself to be accepted as a full-fledged member of the village when he joins the *Catsinamu (Catcina* Society).

It had been a hard year altogether for Sarah and Stewart. Pauline's wedding, although such a great event for the family, had made a big dent in the budget because so many goods were now purchased from the store and big bills had accumulated there. Stewart's pay check was spent before it even had a chance to get to Sarah, paying for the truck, the gasoline bill, the electricity bill now that the Department of the Interior had brought electricity to the village, and all the expenses created by two children in school.

The money problems had brought even more tension between Sarah and Stewart. She had to struggle so much all alone week after week as Stewart worked in town to make ends meet. Tsokavo's death had been the straw that broke the camel's back; the family had not been the same since the awful tragedy.

It was late on Saturday night, perhaps eleven o'clock or more, and Sarah, exhausted by a long day of washing at the laundry the Indian Service had built near the store way below Second Mesa, was aimlessly turning the pages of a Montgomery Ward catalog that Pauline had brought from town one day. Her eyes had been getting worse lately. She needed glasses badly but somehow never found the time to go to the Indian Hospital in Keams Canyon, the Hopi agency town fifteen miles away. Besides, she had to ask someone for a ride, and she did not like to ask.

Outside, a cold wind was driving snowflakes into the village from the direction of Flagstaff when she heard the truck. Stewart had finally come home safely. Putting the catalog away, along with all the dreams their color pages brought into her mind, she put the coffee pot on the stove.

Without a word, Stewart brought in several brown paper bags, the week's dirty laundry and put a box of doughnuts on the table.

"I thought it would go well with our coffee tonight," he said.

"Did you have a hard week?"

"A terrible one," was his answer. "They had two derailments between Flagstaff and Kingman this week, and we had to repair the line. The weather! ...lots of snow."

"My husband, did you remember this weekend was *Suskahimu* day?"

"Yes, I did," Stewart answered, a tired look on his face. "In fact, I bought an assortment of paints and brushes for Suma. He has been wanting them to do his artwork."

Stewart brought a package he had unloaded with the rest from the truck minutes before and put it on the table in front of Sarah.

"Oh! It is really nice, Stewart. I see you have thought about our boy; it makes me feel really good." Sarah looked at her husband and smiled.

Since Tsokavo's death, they rarely shared an intimate moment like this talking about their boy, afraid that it might bring painful memories.

"Potiwa came today to inquire about the ceremony. He wants to take his ceremonial son to the kiva tomorrow night."

"That will be all right."

"So, if you agree, I will let him know tomorrow morning, so we can all be ready when the sun goes down to the other side."

After sundown Suma's ceremonial father, selected long beforehand for the initiation ceremony into the *Catcinamu*, would take his ceremonial son to the kiva. Suma's natural father and mother and other relatives would go with them. Then three *Catcinas*, one *Tumas* and two *Tunwup Catcinas* (whipping *Catcinas*) would administer the ceremonial whipping or cleansing ceremony for purification purposes.

As they enter the kiva, the whipping *Catcinas* administer the whipping, first to the parents who claim that they don't want their children to be whipped with yucca strips and offer to be whipped instead, which the *Catcinas* will do but will also whip ceremonially the children to be initiated as this ceremony is considered to be a purification ritual.

After the whole ritual takes place, and for the first time, the newly initiated young boys and girls will be told that *Catcinas* are not spiritual entities but men of the village who personify the spirit being. They are also told that long, long ago, the spirit beings called *Catcinas* lived among the people, but now they have retreated to their spirit home, and it is the custom for them to be represented by the men of the village. They are ultimately told never to reveal this to younger children.

Stewart gave a sigh of relief.

"I am glad you can do all that, Sarah. With me working in town, it makes it so difficult to take care of my ceremonial duties."

Sarah bowed her head as the compliment was rightfully given to her by her husband, acknowledging it in the customary humble way as Hopi women have done for so many centuries.

"We'd better go to bed, Stewart, tomorrow will be a long day again as we prepare ourselves for the ceremony."

"Yes, I know but let me tell you something, Sarah. I feel good about our boy being initiated; it is as if all our efforts are really worth it. It is as if our Hopi way is being perpetuated through our children and in this way will live forever.

"As the world is seemingly facing more and more serious troubles, just as the prophecies had told us, our Hopi way will bring a constant stream of good, powerful energies which eventually will tip the balance of things."

"Yes, I understand," Sarah acknowledged. "I feel good about it, too. It seems, in fact, that since our son has been steadily preparing himself for his initiation into the *Catcinamu*, we all have been happier as if the *Catcinas* themselves were looking at us with pride because we are protecting our old ways."

"You know, Sarah," Stewart said, seemingly giving a last statement before going to bed, "the Hopi way is really the best for us, and it is what has kept us together through it all."

PAYIK'ALA
The Three Horned Catcina

The village harbored an air of deep powerful mystery as the bright orange disk of the Arizona sun was disappearing behind the San Francisco peaks at the end of the next day. A deeply mystical feeling was taking over as all the families who had children to be initiated that night were making their way to the kivas.

The square, fortress-like shapes of the kivas with their long ladders pointing straight at the darkening sky, are a powerful reminder to the Hopis that right there, just below ground, lives a most powerful mystique that has endured for untold centuries. And being part of it gives the sense of belonging to the earth itself, never alone, never abandoned, never forgotten.

In reverent silence each family was progressing toward its respective kiva. In the coolness of the evening breeze, the women pushed their shawls to cover their mouths, the men bending toward the earth that saw them emerge, untold centuries ago during the first, second, third, and fourth emergences into this physical world.

Right on top of the roof of Stewart's kiva, the *Catcinas* were waiting, the *Mana Catcina* (female *Catcina*) and the two *Tunwup* whipping *Catcinas*.

"What do you want from us?" Stewart asked them.

"We have come to whip the children who are bad," was the answer.

"We do not want our children to be whipped."

"But we have to do it."

"Then whip us first."

As Stewart said that, he bent forward so the *Catcina* could administer the four ceremonial lashes on his back with the yucca
bunches he held in his hands. Every member of the family did the
same until finally Suma's ceremonial father submitted to the ritual,
and putting a pinch of cornmeal in the *Catcina*'s hand, asked him in that
way to do the same to his ceremonial son.

Everyone came down the kiva ladder to take his place among the
other families who were having a child being initiated that night.

The intense heat from the potbelly stove, the flimsy light of the
kerosene lamp, combined with the acrid smell of the kiva priest's
pipe smoking Hopi tobacco was adding to the highly mystical event
soon to take place in the kiva.

As silence set in over the family members sitting in the back of
the kiva, the boys and girls to be initiated were held by their ceremonial fathers on the other side. The three officiating *Catcinas* asked
permission to enter the kiva, and the priest standing at the foot of the
ladder answered in a loud voice: "What do you want?" he said.

"We want to come to whip the children who are bad."

"Then you have to whip me first."

"We cannot do that, you are the priest!"

"It does not matter, you'll have to whip me first."

As the holy ceremonial masked entities came down the ladder and
stood at the foot of it, they made the motions of whipping the kiva
priest and moved toward the area where ceremonial fathers and their
now-really-frightened children had taken seats on the kiva benches.

Each sponsor of a boy to be initiated undressed him carefully, the
girls being allowed to keep their black mantas on. Putting a pinch of
cornmeal in the whipping *Catcina*'s left hand, each ceremonial father
asked in that same manner that his ceremonial son be whipped four
times to be purified before being accepted as a member of the *Catcina*

society.

The children's frightened cries, along with the ritual protests of their guardians, created a tense moment as the ritual of purification went on.

As finally it ended, the priest blessed the *Catcinas* with the smoke from his kiva pipe and the cornmeal from the bag suspended from his neck, and they departed swiftly up the ladder that had first brought them in.

They would circle the kiva four times before finally disappearing in the secretness of the night, having performed once more the ancient ritual that had been brought through the channel of the centuries, generation after generation of Hopi men and women conscious of their ancestral duties as members of their own people and of the human race at large.

In the kivas, little boys and little girls would be instructed in their new roles as full-fledged members of the village, now that they knew who and what the *Catcinas* really were. The boys would be entitled to train for the masked dances now, and the girls would learn their duties as future mothers and family heads of the Hopi household.

In this way the tradition of the Hopi would never be lost and with them would live the long chain of events that connect them with their beginnings, fully aware of *who they are, what they are for* and *what they should do about it.*

As Sarah, Stewart and their family made their way toward the house in the dead of the night, a renewed hope made its way into the very fibers of their family life through which all the sufferings, the joys and the price they had to pay for it made all the sense in the world.

TASAP CATCINA
Navajo Catcina

The following morning a resplendent rising sun blessed the Hopi desert as it would do until the end of time, bringing with the warmth of its rays the creative energy which makes everything grow.

Kotsamana and Makto will watch its path season after season from the top of their mesa home; the *Catcinas* will come and go, helping the people to grasp what it takes to be a Hopi.

If the prophecies tell the truth, and so far they have, intruders and their pervading ways will also come and go, leaving the people of the high mesas confronted by, nourished with and secured into the self-sufficiency of "the Hopi Way."

From the big window of the new home Makto had completed the previous summer, the young couple watched the rising sun. Pauline had arranged their few pieces of furniture in such a way that they would be able, each morning, to see the great mystery of sunrise, the blessing of the new day. Without exchanging a word, their thoughts united in silence.

So many things, Pauline thought, so many things.

The new baby, the need for cash, the death of Tsokavo, the new house. Makto wants to be the farmer his father taught him to be. I know he will do well, but even so it will not pay for the baby's things: bills, groceries, schooling. Working as a waitress at the Cultural Center will get us nowhere, but I have to do it. My life, Makto's life, the baby's — all these now have their convenient cubbyholes, just like the Hopi ceremonies that now must wait for weekends in order to bring the gods back to life in the village.

Everyone working. The old days, the old calendar changed by this new regimen of work, work, work. I make plaques and baskets like mother, but these I must sell to Pahanas at the Hopi Arts and Crafts Center.

My poor brother, safe from harm among the cloud people. No, he is not poor any more; the white rocks of his grave upon which sat the Hopi bowls of food so he would not grow hungry on his journey. The food is long since gone, the sandy hill below Mishongnovi with its heavy blanket of white stones and wildflowers, windswept. I feel no confusion about my brother. He lived, he is gone. He is still alive, but not here. Like Kwahu, the eagle brother who lives on our family roof, and was the summer night friend of restless Tsokavo who would join him up there, the spirit of eagle and eagle's brother, my brother Tsokavo, join and cross the threshold of time. Both will protect us.

I think, now, of all the eagles on all the Hopi rooftops: winged guardians. In the folds of their great wings lies our protection.

This will protect us when nothing else will. And the dawn sun rises high over the minds of Hopis and eagles alike.

ANGWUSNASOMTAKA
Crow Mother
A Figure of Great Dignity